The Action Learning Handbook

To our family and the late Roger Gaunt